CONTENTS

FAST FOOD WITH FLAIR

Behold the Crunchwrap Supreme®. It looks like a gift that's been wrapped in a crispy **tortilla**. Inside there's beef, cheese sauce, lettuce, tomatoes, sour cream, and a crunchy **tostada** shell. But this gift is not meant to be unwrapped. Just take a bite. It magically holds together as you eat.

This well-known menu item sums up the kind of food you'll find at Taco Bell®. The restaurant offers American versions of Mexican food, and it adds some flair to basic ingredients.

FAVORITE FOOD FRANCHISES

TACO BELL®

Laura Purdie Salas

Mitchell Lane
PUBLISHERS

Parent and Caregiver Tips for Creating Nonfiction Readers

The high-interest topics in the ***Favorite Food Franchises*** series are sure to get your young reader excited about reading nonfiction. While exploring a fascinating subject, your reader will be introduced to new facts, ideas, and vocabulary.

Tips for Reading Nonfiction

Talk about Nonfiction
Explain that nonfiction books provide facts about real-world topics. When readers read nonfiction, they gain a rich understanding of the world. They build background knowledge that provides a foundation for learning and academic success.

Look at the Parts
This book contains the following helpful features. Share the purpose of each feature with your reader.

Photos, Captions, and Graphic Aids
The photos, captions, maps, diagrams, time lines, and other graphic aids in nonfiction texts contain a wealth of information. Help your reader identify different ways information can be displayed.

Sidebars
These extra tidbits of information help satisfy readers' curiosity and expand their knowledge.

Table of Contents
Located at the front of the book, this list shows the big ideas within the text and the page numbers where they can be found.

Glossary
Located at the back of the book, the glossary defines key words and phrases that are related to the topic. These words and phrases can be found in the text in colored type.

Comprehension Questions (Fact Check)
Multiple-choice questions help readers self-check to make sure they understand what they read.

Index
Located at the back of the book, the index is an alphabetical list of topics and the page numbers where they can be found.

With a little help and guidance, your reader will be on their way to enjoying and learning from nonfiction books.

Mitchell Lane
PUBLISHERS
mitchelllanepub.com

2001 SW 31st Avenue
Hallandale, FL 33009

First Edition, 2025.
Author: Laura Purdie Salas
Designer: Rhea Magaro
Editor: Kim Thompson

Series: Favorite Food Franchises
Title: Taco Bell / by Laura Purdie Salas

Hallandale, FL : Mitchell Lane Publishers, [2025]

Library bound ISBN: 979-8-89260-314-0
Paperback ISBN: 979-8-89260-438-3
eBook ISBN: 979-8-89260-316-4

PHOTO CREDITS
Alamy: Mahmoud Masad, cover, 1; John Muggenborg, 3; Michael Neelon(misc), 5; Allen Creative / Steve Allen, 6; Ira Berger, 7; Jonny White, 12; John Muggenborg, 32; Dreamstime: Brent Hofacker, 22; Public Domain: 24; Shutterstock: dwph, cover; Patricia C. Adams, 1; JasonCameral, 4; Kathy Hutchins, 5; rangizzz, 5, 7, 8, 11, 13, 17, 23, 26; Fevziie, 9; Anne Czichos, 10; Tada Images, 10; Najmi Arif, 11; ColorMaker, 11; melissamn, 12; Ken Wolter, 13; naulicrea, 14; Mihir Doshi, 15; etorres, 16; KucherAV, 17; The Image Party, 18; Halfpoint, 19; rblfmr, 20; Brent Hofacker, 21; Sink artworks, 23; Kathy Hutchins, 24; ARENA Creative, 27; Logan Bush, 29; Taco Bell Corp.: 20, 25, Wikimedia: 21

Adam Richman

Taco-Bout It

Food critic Adam Richman loves the Crunchwrap Supreme. He joked that the person who invented it, the fast-food product developer Lois Carson, should be nominated for a Nobel Prize.

Taco Bell seems eager to please its customers. It opens early and closes late. It's one of the least expensive fast-food restaurants.

Most menu items can be ordered separately. This lets you create the exact meal you want. The company tries out new menu items regularly. That means you'll often find a "limited time only" food to taste.

Taco-Bout It

Taco Bell is the fourth-largest restaurant chain in the United States, serving 42 million customers each week. The company sells more than two billion tacos each year. That's five and a half million tacos every day!

WHO PUT THE BELL IN TACO BELL?

Glen Bell was the **founder** of Taco Bell. In the late 1940s and 1950s, he opened a series of different restaurants in California. During these years, more people were buying cars and cruising around to show them off. Drive-thru restaurants began to open up. Most served burgers and fries.

Bell liked Mexican food. He believed that tacos could compete with hamburgers. He figured out how to cook and serve them up fast. In 1962, he opened the very first Taco Bell in Downey, California. Many customers had never seen tacos before. They called them "tay-kohs." But once people tried them, they loved them.

Taco-Bout It

Bell learned about hard-shell tacos from Mitla Cafe, a neighboring restaurant. Its owners were from Mexico. They were probably the first to sell crispy tacos in the United States. Bell was second.

Taco Bell grew quickly. Within two years, Bell opened eight more Taco Bells. Each one had a grand opening party with searchlights and salsa music.

By 1970, there were 325 **franchises**. In 2024, the company had more than 8,500 restaurants. Several hundred locations are in other countries, but most are in the United States. California, Texas, and Florida have the most Taco Bells.

Portland, OR

New York, NY

Taco-Bout It

Taco Bells in other countries offer some special menu items. Franchises in Spain sell the Chocodilla®. It's a flour tortilla filled with melted chocolate and Kit Kat® candy bar pieces.

TACOS FOR ALL

Taco Bell focuses on digital ordering. Often, you make your selections on a touch screen. You can order ahead and have your food ready for pickup at the drive-thru. People who use the company's app get access to certain foods and deals.

Taco-Bout It

Taco Bell in Brooklyn Park, Minnesota, has an unusual design. Its second-floor kitchen sits above four drive-thru lanes. Completed orders are lowered in clear tubes down to waiting drivers below.

Some customers eat at the restaurant. Early Taco Bells were influenced by Spanish Mission **architecture**. They had features like tile roofs and archways. Newer franchises may have a more urban design with concrete and industrial elements. Some California locations offer many options for outdoor dining.

The company has used some extreme methods to supply its food. People in Bethel, Alaska, heard that a Taco Bell might be coming to their town in 2012. When they found out it wasn't true, they were disappointed. Taco Bell got involved, sending a helicopter to airlift a truck into Bethel. The truck contained the ingredients to make 10,000 tacos.

In 2023, Taco Bell wanted to help people celebrate "Taco Tuesday." It gave away free tacos every Tuesday for a month. It also contributed five million dollars toward people's orders from Mexican restaurants across the U.S.

TACO Tuesday

LIMITED INGREDIENTS, UNLIMITED OPTIONS

Most Taco Bell items are made up of the same ingredients combined in different ways. These include beans, beef, chicken, cheese, lettuce, sauces, and shells.

A lawsuit once claimed that Taco Bell didn't put enough beef in its "seasoned beef." The lawsuit was dropped after the company revealed that the ingredient is mostly beef. Cooks at a central location start with meat, but they add seasonings and fillers like oats. Then, the frozen or **dehydrated** mixture is shipped to individual restaurants.

Taco-Bout It

Taco Bell is a favorite of customers who don't eat meat. The company has at least 30 vegetarian or vegan ingredients that can be combined in hundreds of different ways.

Approximately 60 people work at Taco Bell's **Innovation** Kitchen. They come up with thousands of ideas for new menu items. They consider how foods look, how much crunch they have, and how messy they are to eat.

Each year, the food scientists develop and test around 70 items. About 10 of those items make it onto the menu. Popular items like Nacho Fries and the Crunchwrap Supreme have come from the Innovation Kitchen. Not all new items are a success, though. Taco shells made from blue corn and a seafood salad quickly dropped off the menu.

Taco Bell partners with other brands to spice up its menu and surprise customers. Doritos® Locos Tacos have a shell made out of a big Dorito chip. The company tested a Cheez-It® Crunchwrap with a giant Cheez-It cracker inside.

Want a sweet treat after your spicy meal? Cinnabon Delights® are fried dough balls filled with creamy icing and rolled in cinnamon sugar. But watch out: A 12-pack contains over a thousand calories and 52 grams of sugar.

CINNABON®

FIRE SAUCE
I knew you'd come back for me
LIVE MÁS
TACO BELL
VERDE SALSA
I work well with others
MILD SAUCE
Leave no dare undone
Will you marry me?

THE REBEL BELL

Taco Bell has always been a bit **rebellious**. It's not afraid to try new things. That's part of what appeals to young customers. The Breakfast Crunchwrap, for example, has a hash brown wrapped up inside the tortilla. A Halloween-themed taco, the Black Jack, had a black shell. A company program called the Menu Blast challenges employees to **hack** the menu and come up with creative combinations and innovations.

Taco-Bout It

Taco Bell's sauce packets feature snappy phrases such as *So what if I did?*, *Problem solved*, and *You so get me!* The company offers a program for recycling used packets.

Taco Bell's ads are also out of the ordinary. The company offered to give away free tacos if the falling Mir space station hit a target in the Pacific Ocean. Television host Conan O'Brien visited the Innovation Kitchen. A TikTok musical with pop star Doja Cat was a big hit.

Some ads have not been successful. "Make a Run for the Border" was one unpopular **slogan**. Many people in the Latin American community were insulted.

Doja Cat

Conan O'Brien

LeBron James and Jason Sudeikis in a Taco Tuesday commercial

Hayley Kiyoko wearing the Taco Bell x Wildfang coverall with pockets shaped to fit popular menu items

The company runs the Taco Bell Foundation to help others. The charity focuses on college scholarships and career training. It's donated more than 155 million dollars since 1992.

Taco Bell is known for taking risks and being honest about both successes and failures. Luckily, its efforts to help others are a big success!

Taco-Bout It

Customers can give to the foundation by rounding up. If they pay five dollars for an order that costs $4.78, the extra 22 cents goes to the foundation. In this way, more than 41 million dollars were donated in 2023.

A TACO BELL TIME LINE

1951 Glen Bell develops his version of a crispy taco. It's based on the tacos at Mitla Cafe.

1962 Bell opens the first Taco Bell in Downey, California.

1967 The 100th Taco Bell opens.

1992 The Taco Bell Foundation begins partnering with the Boys & Girls Clubs of America.

1995 Taco Bell sponsors the first X Games, showcasing extreme sports.

2004 PepsiCo develops the menu item Mountain Dew Baja Blast® just for Taco Bell.

2006 The Crunchwrap Supreme joins the permanent menu.

2010 Glen Bell dies from Parkinson's disease.

2018 Nacho Fries have the best sales of any new product in Taco Bell's history. Taco Bell creates a futuristic restaurant for Comic-Con.

2023 Taco Bell sues another restaurant and wins the right to use the phrase "Taco Tuesday."

2024 Taco Bell opens The Cantinas, an "early retirement community" for the "old at heart." Guests can play pickleball, go to bed early, and celebrate the "laid back spirit in everyone."

GLOSSARY

architecture (AHR-ki-tek-chur)
a style of building; the way that a building is designed

dehydrated (dee-HYE-dray-tid)
with all the water removed; dried out to slow spoilage and make transportation easier

founder (FOUN-dur)
the person who starts a company or organization

franchises (fran-CHYE-sis)
individual locations of a chain store or restaurant; legal agreements that let people run businesses that sell products created by a larger company

hack (hak)
to find clever tips or techniques for improving something

innovation (in-uh-VAY-shuhn)
a new idea or method

rebellious (ri-BEL-yuhs)
resistant to or disrespectful of authority; rule-breaking

slogan (SLOH-guhn)
a short phrase a company uses in its advertising

tortilla (tor-TEE-yuh)
a round, flat bread that is made from flour or cornmeal and that is often used in Mexican cooking

tostada (toe-STAH-duh)
a tortilla that is deep-fried and crunchy

FACT CHECK

1. The Taco Bell Foundation focuses on ____.
   A. health B. education C. music

2. Taco Bell sauce packets are unusual because of their ____.
   A. sayings B. ingredients C. colors

3. Taco Bell sometimes features other ____ in their products.
   A. cities B. brands C. celebrities

4. Taco Bell began in ____.
   A. Texas B. Mexico C. California

Answers: 1. B, 2. A, 3. B, 4. C

FURTHER READING

Cohn, Jessica. *On the Job in a Restaurant*. South Egremont, MA: Red Chair Press, 2016.

Lowe, Lindsey. *Mexican Culture and Cooking*. New York: Cavendish Square, 2023.

Melian, Gaby. *Gaby's Latin American Kitchen: 70 Kid-Tested and Kid-Approved Recipes for Young Chefs*. Boston: America's Test Kitchen Kids, 2022.

ON THE INTERNET

Biz Kid$: Young Entrepreneur Profiles
https://bizkids.com/groups/profiles
Learn about young people who have started their own companies.

Food Network: Cooking with Kids
https://www.foodnetwork.com/recipes/packages/recipes-for-kids/cooking-with-kids
Find recipes from the network for fun in the kitchen.

Old El Paso: Kid-Friendly Mexican Recipes
https://www.oldelpaso.com/articles/kid-friendly-mexican-recipes
Learn to make something delicious.

INDEX

ABOUT THE AUTHOR

Laura Purdie Salas is an award-winning author who lives and writes in Minnesota. Her many books include poetry and nonfiction. Laura loves to read, play board games, knit, explore nature, and spend time with her husband and two daughters. She also eats way too much fast food and is a regular at Taco Bell! Her usual order is a Doritos Locos Taco, two Cinnabon Delights, and a Zero-Sugar Baja Blast. Visit Laura at laurasalas.com.